PEGASUS ENCYCLOPEDIA LIBRARY

Food and Nutrition

NUTRITION

Edited by: Pallabi B. Tomar, Hitesh Iplani
Managing editor: Tapasi De
Designed by: Vijesh Chahal, Anil Kumar, Rohit Kumar
Illustrated by: Suman S. Roy, Tanoy Choudhury
Colouring done by: Vinay Kumar, Kiran Kumari & Pradeep Kumar

CONTENTS

What is nutrition? 3

History 5

Types of nutrients 7

What is malnutrition? 10

What is plant nutrition? 12

What is animal nutrition? 14

What is human nutrition? 15

What is sports nutrition? 17

Processed foods 19

Why is proper nutrition important? 20

Dangers of poor nutrition 23

Nutrition & life cycles 26

Tips for a healthy diet 29

Test Your Memory 31

Index 32

What is nutrition?

Nutrition is the science that studies the process by which living organisms acquire all the things that are necessary for them to live and grow. Nutrition focuses on the role of nutrients, which are defined as substances that the body cannot make on its own and include things like vitamins, minerals and certain macromolecules. Basically, nutrition consists of diet (what you take in) and metabolism (what happens to it after it enters your body).

Food taken in any form either solid or liquid supplies the body a means to produce energy of any form. The available nutrition in the food promotes growth and maintenance of the body. Proper nutrition is only possible when the diet taken is balanced and the food consumed contains all the basic nutrients.

No single food is rich in all the nutrients so a variety of food should be included to fulfil all the requirements of the body as far as nutrients are concerned. When the food consumed does not fulfil the requirements of nutrients, it leads to malnutrition or under nutrition.

Astonishing fact

Most likely due to poor nutrition as children, many Greeks and Romans were shorter than people today. Men from Pompeii, for example, averaged 5 ft 5½ inches and women averaged 5 ft 2 inches.

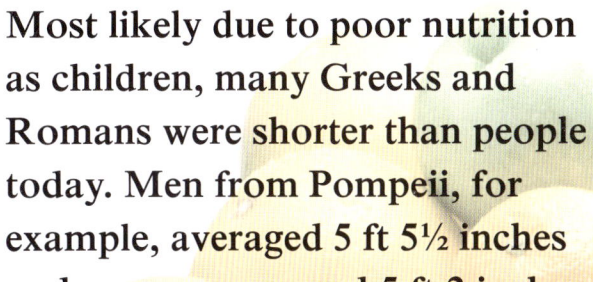

NUTRITION

Good nutrition requires a satisfactory diet, which is capable of supporting the individual consuming it, in a state of good health by providing the desired nutrients in the required amounts. It must provide the right amount of fuel to execute normal physical activity. If the total amount of nutrients provided in the diet is insufficient, a state of under nutrition will develop.

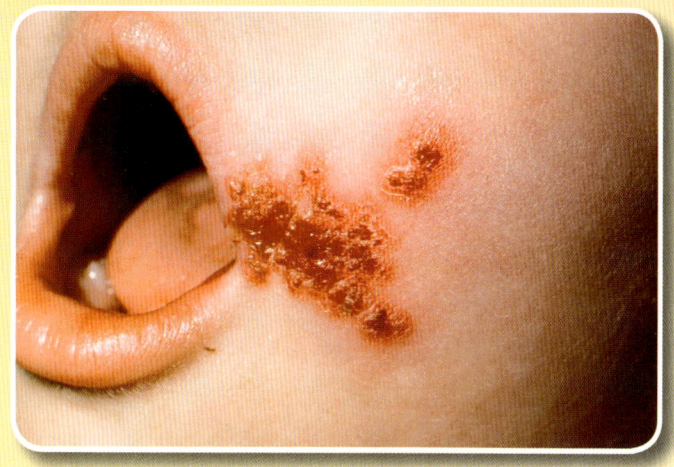

Astonishing fact

The English are sometimes called 'limeys' because British sailors would eat limes to stave off scurvy. Limes were later replaced by lemons due to the lack of adequate vitamin C in lime juice.

Nutrition also focuses on how diseases, conditions and problems can be prevented or lessened with a healthy diet.

Nutrition also involves identifying how certain diseases, conditions or problems maybe caused by dietary factors, such as poor diet (malnutrition), food allergies, metabolic diseases, etc.

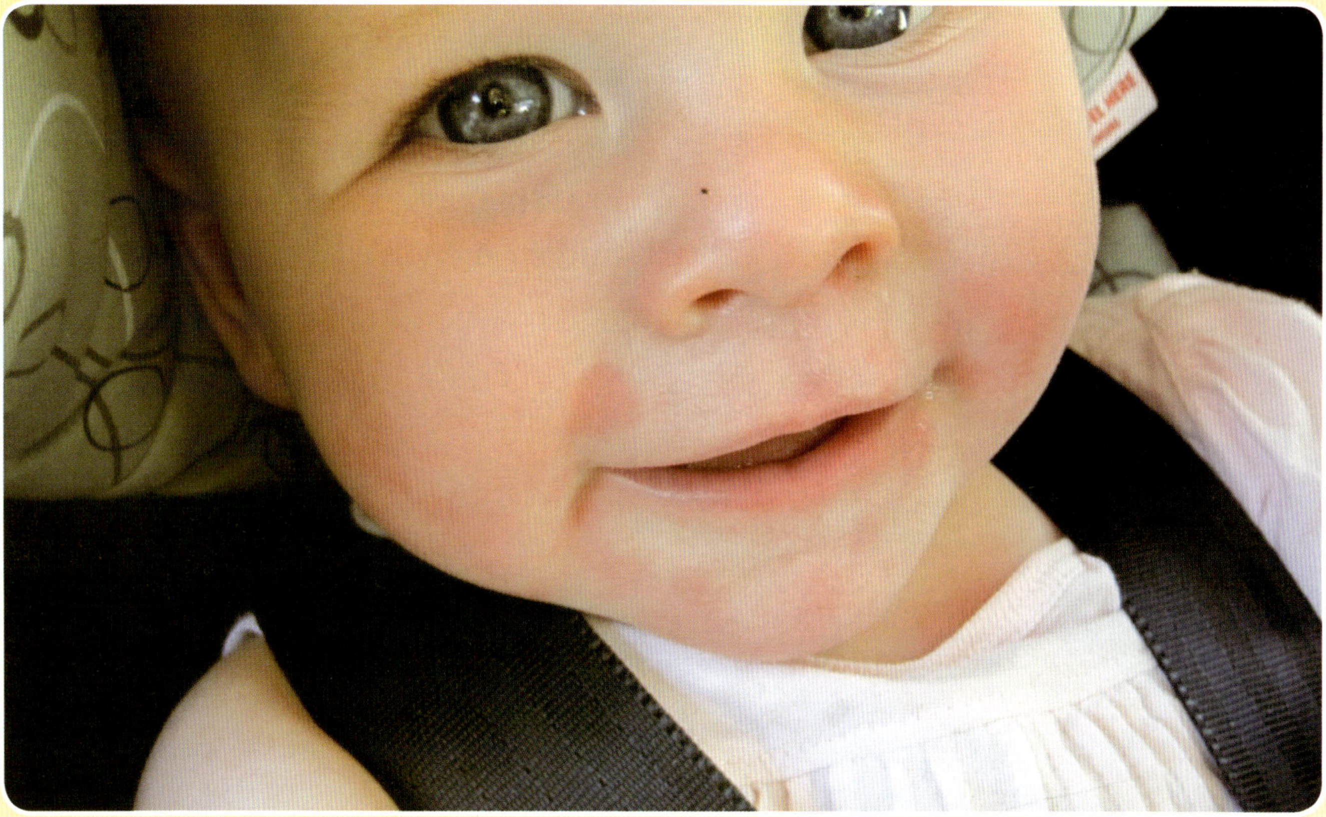

History

The history of the study of food as medicine reveals centuries of discovery and development. Although, modern science and the latest discoveries in biology, medicine and health inform today's field of nutrition and diet, people have been investigating the very real link between food and health since ancient times.

In 400 B.C. the Greek physician Hippocrates said, 'Let thy food be thy medicine and thy medicine be thy food.' Hippocrates realized that food impacts a person's health, body and mind to help prevent illness as well as maintain wellness.

In Hippocrates' Greece, as well as across pre-modern Europe and Asia since ancient times, foods were used to affect health. For instance, Garlic was used to cure athlete's foot and eating ginger was thought to stimulate the metabolism.

Dr. James Lind

In 1747, a British Navy physician, Dr. James Lind, saw that sailors were developing scurvy, a deadly bleeding disorder, on long voyages. He observed that they ate only non-perishable foods such as bread and meat. Lind's experiment fed one group of sailors' salt water, one group with vinegar and one group limes. Those given limes didn't develop scurvy. And although Vitamin C wasn't discovered until the 1930s, this experiment changed the way physicians thought about food.

Astonishing fact

Vitamin D is unusual because it is the only vitamin that can be synthesized in the body. Sunlight is the main source of Vitamin D.

NUTRITION

During the Enlightenment and into the Victorian age, scientific and medical development increased rapidly. The concept of metabolism, the transfer of food and oxygen into heat and water in the body, creating energy, was discovered in 1770 by Antoine Lavoisier. And in the early 1800s, the importance of the elements of carbon, nitrogen, hydrogen and oxygen the main components of food, were recognised as being essential to health.

In 1912, E.V. McCollum, a US Department of Agriculture researcher at the University of Wisconsin, began using rats instead of humans in his experiments rather than cows and sheep. He found the first fat-soluble vitamin, Vitamin A,

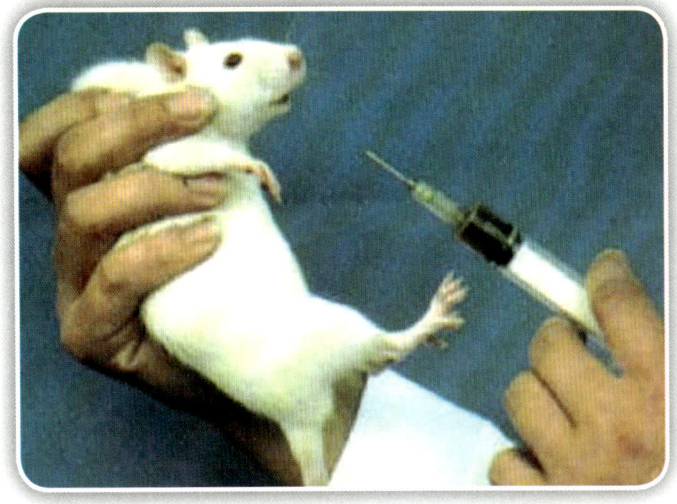

and discovered that rats were healthier when they were fed butter rather than lard, as butter contains more Vitamin A. Other diseases were linked to vitamin deficiencies, such as beri-beri, resulting from a lack of Vitamin B and rickets, brought on by a lack of Vitamin D.

Many other vitamins were discovered and isolated in the early 20th century and the concept of supplementing health with vitamins was born. The first vitamin pills were marketed in the 1930s and created a new industry around science-based health products.

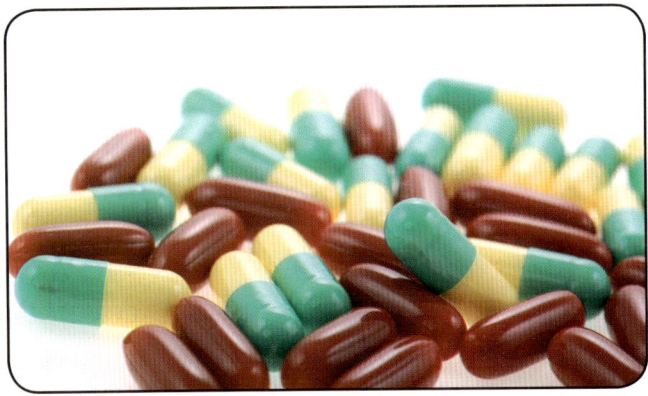

Astonishing fact

The term 'vitamin' was coined by Polish-American chemist Casimir Funk and is derived from vital (necessary for life) and amine (a compound containing nitrogen and hydrogen).

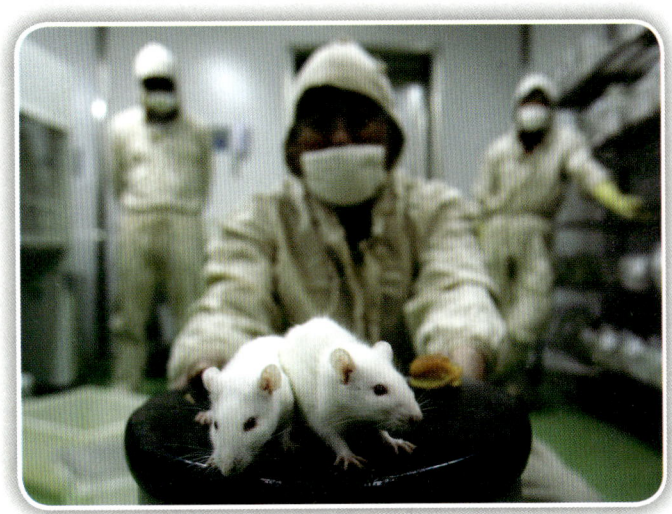

Types of nutrients

The body breaks down the foods we eat in order to use nutrients found in these items. While many people focus on eating healthy foods in order to maintain a healthy weight, not getting the proper nutrients can cause problems beyond weight gain. There are six types of nutrients the body needs to survive.

Astonishing fact

Salt is the most common seasoning mentioned in the Bible. Salt is a vital mineral that is not only essential to life, but also preserves other foods critical for survival.

Rice

Carbohydrates

Carbohydrates are primarily responsible for fuelling your body, giving you energy throughout the day. Some carbohydrates, like table sugar, are broken down very quickly for quick bursts of energy, while other carbohydrates, like whole grains are more complex. Complex carbohydrates take longer to break down and thus fuel you with energy slowly throughout the day. Foods high in carbohydrate include fruits, sweets, soft drinks, breads, pastas, beans, potatoes, bran, rice and cereals.

Fats

Fats are our storehouses of energy. When we have excess nutrients in our body, some of it is stored as fat. The primary purpose of fat is energy production. There are two main types of fats—saturated and unsaturated. Animal fats (meat, butter, lard) are usually saturated fats and contribute to heart disease and cancer. Vegetable fats (olive oil, corn oil) are generally unsaturated fats and are less harmful. Some fats have been found to be helpful in preventing some cancers and heart disease. These fats called omega-3 fatty acids are found in some fish, especially cold-water fish.

Fish

NUTRITION

Proteins

Proteins provide the body with material to grow. Where carbohydrates and fats are broken down to produce energy, protein is broken down to give your body material for tissue repair and growth. Common protein rich foods can include milk, soy milk, eggs, cheese, yogurt, peanut butter, lean meats, fish and poultry, beans, tofu, lentils and other legumes, grains, including bread and pasta, nuts and seeds.

Minerals

Minerals are compounds, obtained from your diet, that combine in several ways to form the structures of your body. For instance, calcium is a mineral that is crucial in the formation and maintenance of your bones. Minerals also help regulate body functions. Minerals do not produce energy.

Astonishing fact

Salt was so important that it was also often used as a form of currency or as a unit of exchange!

Types of nutrients

Vitamins

Vitamins are substances that your body needs to grow and develop normally. There are 13 vitamins your body needs. They are vitamins A, C, D, E, K and the B vitamins (thiamine, riboflavin, niacin, pantothenic acid, biotin, vitamin B-6, vitamin B-12 and folate). You can usually get all your vitamins from the foods you eat. Your body can also make vitamins D and K.

Each vitamin has specific jobs. If you have low levels of certain vitamins, you may develop a deficiency disease. For example, if you don't get enough vitamin D, you could develop rickets. Some vitamins may help prevent medical problems. Vitamin A prevents night blindness.

Water

Water is, perhaps, the most critical nutrient. We can live without other nutrients for several weeks, but we can go without water for only about a week. The body needs water to carry out all of its life processes. Watery solutions help dissolve other nutrients and carry them to all the tissues. The chemical reactions that turn food into energy or tissue-building materials can take place only in a watery solution. The body also needs water to carry away waste products and to cool itself.

Astonishing fact

Temperature can affect appetite. A cold person is more likely to eat more food.

NUTRITION

What is malnutrition?

Malnutrition occurs when the body does not get enough nutrients. This can mean not getting enough food overall, which can lead to starvation or can be the lack of a single nutrient, such as Vitamin C deficiency, which can lead to scurvy. Causes of malnutrition include not having enough food to eat, not being able to eat a balanced diet, having medical problems that prevent food from being absorbed properly or having psychological problems, such as anorexia nervosa (loss of appetite).

Symptoms of malnutrition vary according to the type of malnutrition and the severity of the problem. If an individual's malnutrition is mild, the person may not show any symptoms at all. General symptoms of this condition can include dizziness, tiredness or weight loss. A person should contact a physician when the individual experiences fainting or hair loss.

The problem is more difficult in areas of widespread poverty or famine. First, there may not be adequate supplies of food. Second, people may not have the money to purchase food that is available. Third, there may not be enough doctors and physicians available to treat not only malnutrition, but any underlying causes beyond lack of food that may be leading to this condition.

Malnutrition is the largest single contributor to disease, according to the UN's Standing Committee on Nutrition (SCN).

> The word 'health' comes from the Anglo-Saxon term 'hal' meaning 'wholeness'.

Astonishing fact
The human digestive system is home to between 10 and 100 trillion bacteria, at least 10 times the amount of cells in the body!

What is malnutrition?

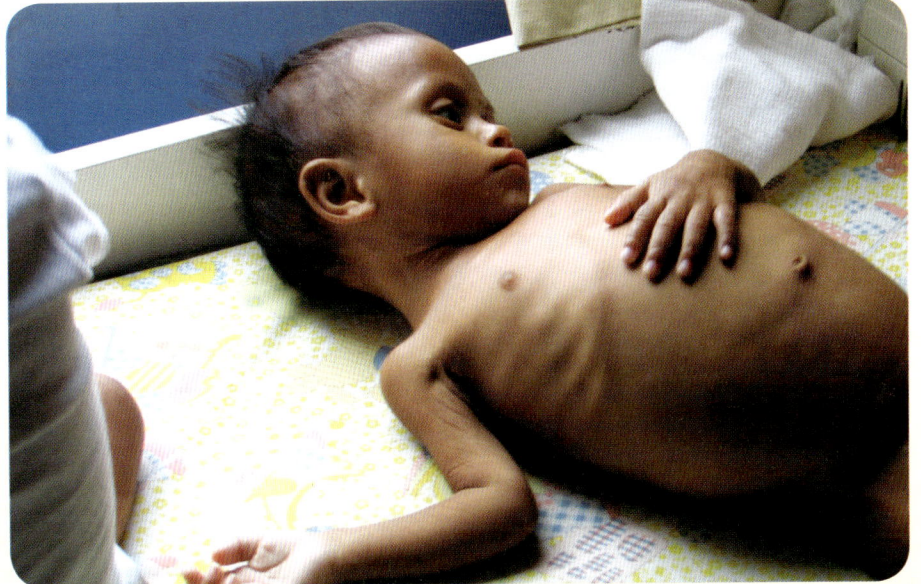

Malnutrition at an early age leads to reduced physical and mental development during childhood. Stunting, for example, affects more than 147 million pre-schoolers in developing countries, according to SCN's World Nutrition Situation 5th report. Iodine deficiency is the world's greatest single cause of mental retardation and brain damage.

Malnutrition can occur because of the lack of a single vitamin in the diet or it can be because a person isn't getting enough food. Starvation is a form of malnutrition. Malnutrition also occurs when adequate nutrients are consumed in the diet, but one or more nutrients are not digested or absorbed properly.

Malnutrition may be mild enough to show no symptoms. However, in some cases it may be so severe that the damage done is irreversible, even though the individual survives.

Worldwide, malnutrition continues to be a significant problem, especially among children who cannot fend adequately for themselves. Poverty, natural disasters, political problems and war, all contribute to conditions, even epidemics of malnutrition and starvation, and not just in developing countries.

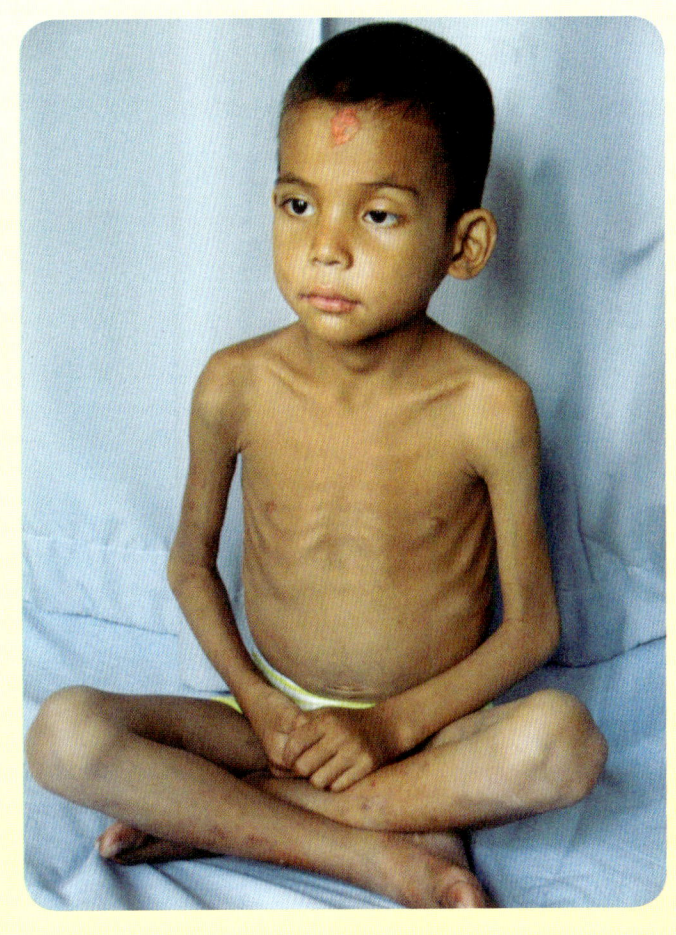

NUTRITION

What is plant nutrition?

Plants need 17 elements for normal growth. Carbon, hydrogen, and oxygen are found in air and water. Nitrogen, potassium, magnesium, calcium, phosphorous and sulphur are found in the soil. These six elements are used in relatively large amounts by the plant and are called **macronutrients**. There are eight other elements that are used in much smaller amounts and are called **micronutrients** or trace elements. The micronutrients which are found in the soil are iron, zinc, molybdenum, manganese, boron, copper, cobalt, and chlorine. All 17 elements, both macronutrients and micronutrients are essential for plant growth.

A balanced nutrition program is essential if plants are to grow and yield to their maximum potential. Adequate nutrition will ensure the plants are structurally strong with increased vigour, giving increased resistance to the penetration of fungal organisms and the possibility to organize their defence mechanisms.

An adequate supply of **nitrogen** is important, as it is essential in the formation of amino acids, which are the building blocks for proteins. Conversely, a surplus of nitrogen leads to overly lush growth, with the soft tissue produced being more open to to disease.

What is plant nutrition?

Phosphorus is essential for a multiplicity of plant functions and it can be replaced by no other element. It is involved in photosynthesis, energy transfer and storage, respiration, cell division and cell enlargement. Phosphorus promotes early root formation and growth, it hastens maturity and it contributes to disease resistance in plants.

Potassium is a vital element and again cannot be replaced by anything else. For plants to produce high yields, particularly of fruits, it is probably of greater importance than nitrogen. It is involved in many processes in the plant including

photosynthesis and respiration, activating enzymes and controlling reaction rates within the plant. It is important in protein synthesis, ionic balance, cell turgidity and root development, increasing winter hardiness and disease resistance in plants.

Sulphur also plays an important role in plant growth and health. It is essential for chlorophyll formation and aids in the production of enzymes and vitamins, which are vital for vigorous, healthy, plants.

Astonishing fact

A deficiency of calcium/Vitamin D during infancy or childhood results in rickets (deformed bones). The bones can become so weak that they can't withstand the body's weight, causing bow legs or knock knees. Once malformed, bones cannot be straightened.

13

NUTRITION

What is animal nutrition?

Animal nutrition incorporates fodder and crop production, fodder conservation, also feed manufacture and the quality control of feeds. Quality of the animal-origin foods is affected mainly by quality of the animal feeds and therefore this latter one has crucial importance in human nutrition.

Animals need a variety of nutrients to meet their basic needs. These nutrients include fats and carbohydrates that provide energy, proteins that furnish amino acids, vitamins that serve as co-factors for enzymes and perform other functions, ions required for water balance and for nerve and muscle function, and selected elements that are incorporated into certain molecules synthesized by cells. To determine the levels of nutrients that are needed to sustain normal activities, researchers monitor the relationship between nutrient intake, the levels of nutrients maintained in the body and health.

Astonishing fact

A person usually swallows around 250 times during dinner.

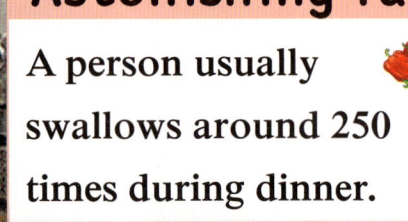

14

What is human nutrition?

Human nutrition is composed of all the materials in the form of food necessary to support life. A healthy diet plays a crucial role in alleviating some health problems such as obesity, cardiovascular disease, diabetes and metabolic syndrome. It also prevents the onset of such deficiency-related diseases like beriberi, scurvy and kwashiorkor. Nutrients come in six major classes.

Human nutrition is the provision to humans to obtain the materials necessary to support life. In general, humans can survive for two to eight weeks without food, depending on stored body fat.

Astonishing fact

Vitamin B12 deficiency can lead to anaemia, neural disorders and psychotic behaviour.

Survival without water is usually limited to three or four days. Lack of food remains a serious problem, with about 36 million humans starving to death every year. Childhood malnutrition is also common and contributes to the global burden of disease. However, global food distribution is not even and obesity among some human populations has increased to almost epidemic proportions, leading to health complications and increased mortality in some developed and a few developing countries. Obesity is caused by consuming more calories than are expended, with many attributing excessive weight gain to a combination of overeating and insufficient exercise.

NUTRITION

Human food contains both vegetables and animals. Both serve in some respects the same purpose in the body, while in others their use is different. Either vegetable or animal food would sustain life, but both together serve much better than either could.

Plant food supplies most of the energy and endurance of the body in starch, sugar and vegetable-oil foods; also much of the body-heat, the food-bulk required for digestive activity, the salts needed for body-regulation, and the water used in living processes and food-utilization. Some vegetable food can also build up body-tissues as it needs repair or material for growth.

The human body contains chemical compounds such as water, carbohydrates, amino acids (in proteins), fatty acids and nucleic acids (DNA and RNA). These compounds in turn consist of elements such as carbon, hydrogen, oxygen, nitrogen, phosphorus, calcium, iron, zinc, magnesium, manganese and so on. All of these chemical compounds and elements occur in various forms and combinations (e.g. hormones, vitamins, phospholipids), both in the human body and in the plant and animal organisms that humans eat.

Astonishing fact

Insects such as termites and ants provide 10 per cent of the protein consumed worldwide. Where insects are an integral part of a diet, they contribute as much as 40 per cent of protein!

What is sports nutrition?

Sports nutrition is a branch of nutritional science which focuses on the unique nutritional needs of athletes. People who want to achieve better athletic performance often need to adjust their diets to meet their physical needs and professional athletes often use the services of an experienced dietician or nutritionist to make sure that their diets are designed appropriately.

Astonishing fact

Some children and pregnant women crave non-nutritive substances such as paint, plaster, rocks and dirt. These cravings may suggest the person lacks certain minerals, such as iron.

Athletes burn a lot of energy, which means that they need to consume more energy than inactive individuals. One of the best sources of energy is carbohydrates, making an increased carbohydrate intake critical for an athlete. Athletes also usually require slightly more protein. They also need the recommended amounts of fruits and vegetables.

Another critical nutritional need for athletes is water consumption. Failure to drink enough water can result in an electrolyte imbalance which can cause medical problems. So, it is important for athletes to integrate water into their dietary plans and to make sure that water is consumed in appropriate amounts at the right intervals, as too much water can also be damaging.

NUTRITION

Different types of athletes have different nutritional needs. Sprinters and marathon runners, for example, require different things from their bodies, and they are also trained differently for races, which mean that their diets will be different. Sports nutrition considers the sport an athlete is involved in and his or her physical condition. Different nutrition may also be involved for training, tapering down after a meet or gearing up for a meet.

Many athletes try to eat food which is healthy, in addition to nutritionally necessary. They may opt for a heavy concentration of fresh foods, for example and try to avoid packaged foods if possible.

Sports clubs and gyms sometimes offer nutrition for sports workshops, which are an excellent resource for information on sports nutrition. Personal trainers can also provide tips and advice, whether people are trying to build muscle for bodybuilding or trim down for rock climbing. Athletes at all levels can also work with nutrition professionals to tailor a diet regimen which will meet their needs, and to learn more about the complex science behind sports nutrition.

Astonishing fact

Improved nutrition has extended the average U.S. lifespan from 30 to 40 years old in the early twentieth century to 70 to 80 years old today.

Processed foods

Food processing is the set of methods and techniques used to transform raw ingredients into food or to transform food into other forms for consumption by humans or animals either in the home or by the food processing industry. Food processing typically takes clean, harvested crops or butchered animal products and uses these to produce attractive, marketable and often long shelf-life food products. Similar processes are used to produce animal feed. The methods used for processing foods include canning, freezing, refrigeration and aseptic processing.

Processed foods usually do not get spoiled soon unlike fresh foods, and are better suited for long distance transportation from the source to the consumer. When they were first introduced some processed foods helped to alleviate food shortages and improved the overall nutrition of populations as it made many new foods available to the masses.

Astonishing fact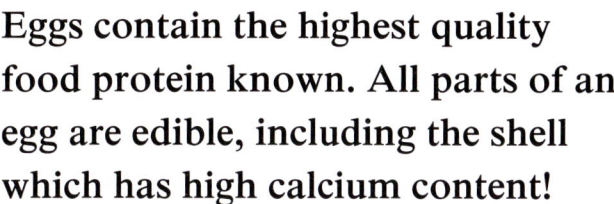

Eggs contain the highest quality food protein known. All parts of an egg are edible, including the shell which has high calcium content!

Another healthy example of food processing is frozen vegetables. While fresh maybe best, freezing vegetables preserves vitamins and minerals and makes them convenient to cook and eat all year around. Fruit and vegetable juice is also an example of a healthy processed food. In fact, some orange juice is fortified with calcium to make it even more nutritious.

Of course, there are a lot of processed foods that aren't good for you. Many processed foods are made with Trans fats, saturated fats and large amounts of sodium and sugar. These types of foods should be avoided or at least eaten sparingly.

NUTRITION

Why is proper nutrition important?

Apart from providing you with energy, nutrition also involves an understanding of how a healthy diet prevents the development of diseases, problems and other conditions of the body.

The foods you eat provide the energy your body needs to function. Just like you need to put fuel in your car or recharge your cell phone battery, your body needs to be fed with energy-providing foods every day. The main energy provider of our body is carbohydrates.

Your body has the easiest time digesting carbohydrates like sugar and starch. Carbohydrates are broken down into individual glucose, fructose or galactose units. Glucose is your body's favourite form of energy. If you don't get enough carbohydrates, your body can make glucose from protein or fat and if you get too many carbohydrates, your body is very good at storing them as fat.

Protein in the foods you eat is broken down into individual amino acids. Your body uses the amino acids to build and repair the various parts of your body. Your muscles contain lots of protein and you need to replenish that protein through your diet. Your body also needs protein for components of your immune system, hormones, nervous system and organs.

Another raw material your body needs is calcium. Calcium has several functions in your body, but its best known as the mineral that is stored in your bones and teeth. You need calcium from your diet to keep your bones and teeth strong.

Your body also needs fats to be healthy. Membranes that contain fats surround all the cells of your body. Your brain has fatty acids and fats are also needed to signal hormones.

Why is proper nutrition important?

You need energy to engage in your daily physical and mental activities. Upon digestion, food that you eat is broken into smaller molecules like glucose, amino acids, fats and vitamins. These molecules and nutrients are the elements that provide your energy.

Among the cells present in your body are egg, bones, fat, muscle, brain, nerve and blood cells. All the cells have functions to perform. The body loses cells and makes new ones. Your body tissues are made up of millions of cells. The nutrients that travel through your bloodstream prevent damage, keep these cells alive and help in producing new ones.

Waste and toxic materials from indigestible food burden your body. A healthy diet should contain lots of fresh fruits and vegetables to cleanse and ease the process of eliminating your waste matter.

You have to take good care of your body because it is a vehicle to transport you from one place to another and to enable you to do the things that you dream of doing. The food that you take in is going to help you to complete your tasks and fulfil all your dreams.

> A person will eat an average of 35 tons of food in his or her lifetime or 1,500 pounds of food a year.

21

NUTRITION

Having good nutrition means eating the right types of foods in the right amounts so that you get all the important nutrients. There are no special diets or particular foods that will boost your immune system. But there are things you can do to keep your immunity up. For example if you are underweight or you have advanced disease you should include more protein as well as extra calories in the form of carbohydrates and fats in your diet.

Astonishing fact

Beets are loaded with vitamins A, B1, B2, B6 and C. The greens have a higher content of iron compared to spinach. They are also an excellent source of calcium, magnesium, copper, phosphorus, sodium and iron.

Proper nutrition means getting all the essential nutrients from your diet that is required to keep your body functioning normally. It is important because there are some important molecules that your body uses to live that it cannot make on its own. The essential nutrients must be obtained in the diet or your body will have a shortage of them. This is critical because your body needs the right amount of all the required molecules to function properly. It is like a string of holiday lights that needs every light to be in place and functioning properly in order to light up; if one light is missing, the whole string loses its beauty. In the same way, if you do not have proper nutrition, your body will lack in one or more essential nutrients and will not be able to function normally.

Dangers of poor nutrition

Nutritional disorders can affect anyone, but most commonly plague the elderly and young children. When the diet does not contain the necessary nutrients and vitamins that are required for the proper functioning of the body's systems, problems may occur within the body. Dysfunctions can result from a nutritional deficiency, which can often be remedied once a change in diet or supplementation is initiated.

Rickets

Rickets can result from a severe deficiency of Vitamin D. It can cause the bones to become soft and malleable which can cause developing bones in children to become deformed. A supplement of vitamin or an increase in foods with high Vitamin D content is advised. Foods high in Vitamin D include salmon, milk products and eggs.

Anaemia

Anaemia is a condition in the body where oxygen can't be utilized through the blood as it should, and the organs and muscles in the body become fatigued. This is because the body is not producing an adequate amount of red blood cells. These blood cells are a necessary component because they help the oxygen get to the body's systems. Anaemia is caused by a depletion of iron in the blood and can be the result of poor diet. Increasing foods into the diet that contain high levels of iron, including liver and clams can alleviate anaemia, as can taking an iron supplement.

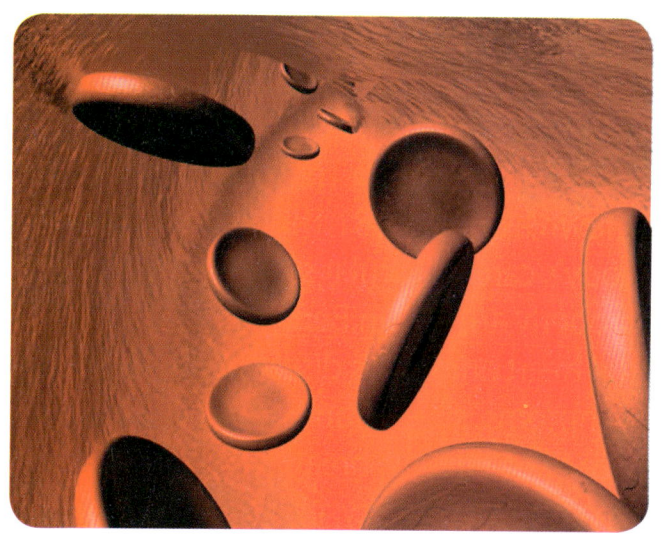

Astonishing fact

One apple on average contains more antioxidants than a large Vitamin C dose of 1,500 mg.

NUTRITION

Scurvy

Scurvy is the result of a vitamin C deficiency. It is becoming more common due to the lack of fresh fruits and vegetables in the modern diet. Scurvy can cause the tissues in the body to disconnect and can lead to severe dental abnormalities and joint problems. To alleviate scurvy, take in more fruits and vegetables into the diet that are high in vitamin C, including oranges, strawberries and bell peppers.

the diet high in vitamin B1, including sunflower seeds, lentils and pinto beans.

Pellagra

Pellagra is a nutritional deficiency that can cause skin disorders in the body, such as dermatitis and psoriasis and mental confusion. It can be the result of eating a diet based heavily on grains, without foods that contain Niacin, such as chicken, beef and salmon. To prevent and alleviate Pellagra, incorporate more meats into the diet.

Beriberi

Beriberi occurs in people that have a severe deficiency in Thiamine, otherwise known as vitamin B1. Thiamine helps the body's cardiovascular system function properly and when Beriberi occurs, the heart and lungs display stressed symptoms, such as an increase in heart rate and difficulty breathing. To treat a Thiamine deficiency, include foods into

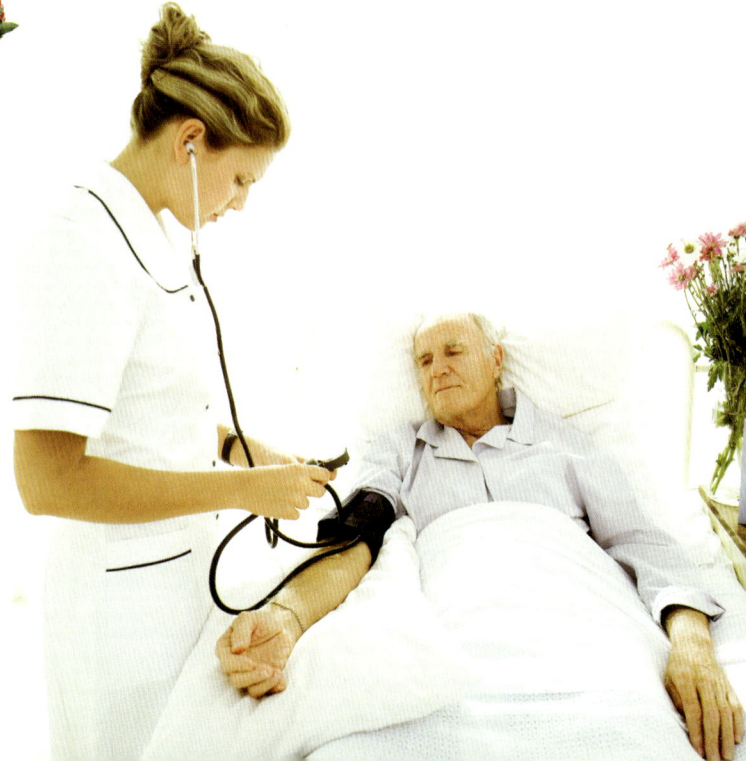

Dangers of poor nutrition

Heart diseases

Coronary heart diseases are a very common health problem and they are closely linked to a diet that is high in unhealthy fats. Decreasing one's intake of fatty foods, especially fried food, will go a long way in preventing heart diseases. On the other hand, a healthy diet chart with an adequate amount of high fibre foods is seen to prevent heart diseases. People who suffer from heart problems are often advised to follow a specific high fibre diet for heart diseases that is rich in raw fruits and vegetables.

In addition to these diseases, conditions such as high cholesterol, high blood pressure, gout and even cancer are affected by the individual's diet.

A balanced diet comprising of diverse and healthy foods is key to promoting good health. After all, we are what we eat. Research continues to prove that eating healthy food promotes good health and unhealthy food habits lead to a diseased body. Foods contain vital nutrients that aid our body's metabolic function. However, a lack of consumption of these nutrients or feeding upon the wrong kinds of food leads to an accumulation of toxins within the body, resulting in chronic diseases in the long run.

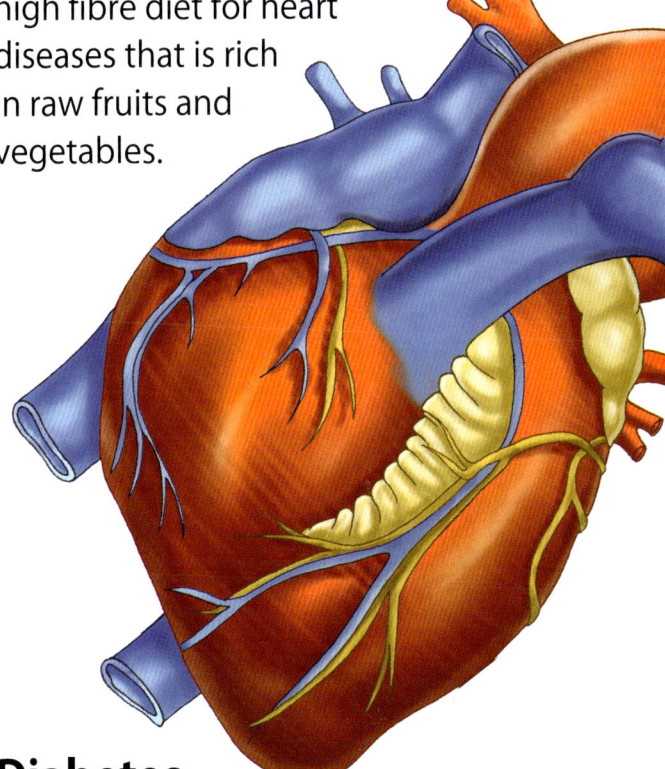

Diabetes

While genetics does play an important role in the onset of diabetes, an unhealthy lifestyle and bad eating habits are also contributing factors. A diabetes diet chart is a diet plan that is high in fibre and low in fat with a minimum amount of saturated fats.

Astonishing fact

Bananas contain everything a human needs and they contain all the 8 amino-acids our body cannot produce itself.

Nutrition & life cycles

Humans require the same nutrients throughout their lifespan. The amount of specific nutrients varies at different stages in the life cycle and varies according to gender, activity level and growth. Certain health conditions and diseases similarly alter nutritional requirements.

Infants: First Year

Infancy is a period of rapid growth and critical nutrition needs. Infants double their birth weight in six months and triple it in one year.

Other nutritional issues during infancy are switching from breast milk or formula to whole milk and solid food, as well as identifying any food allergies.

Toddlers: 1 to 3 Years

Toddlers prefer sweet and salty as they reject bitter and sour foods. Toddlers may reject a new food 5 to 10 times before accepting it, so frequent tasting helps. Children who eat at the table with adults eat more.

Astonishing fact

Colour also plays a role in the food that we eat. Studies have revealed that warm colours like red, orange and yellow seem to cause us to be hungrier.

Nutrition & life cycles

Childhood: 3 to 10 Years

Energy needs change with rapid growth spurts and periods of no growth. Calcium, iron, fluoride and fibre are important nutrients at this stage.

Nutritional risk in children is associated with poverty, diet and the knowledge level of parents. Offer children a variety of healthful foods including fruits and vegetables, whole grains, and proteins in child-sized portions and make mealtime pleasant.

Adolescence: 11 to 20 Years

Protein, vitamins and energy needs related to growth rate and activity level are increased. Adequate supplies of Vitamin D, magnesium and protein are also critical for adolescent growth. Calcium needs are greatest during puberty, but drinking less milk and more sweetened beverages may lower calcium intake. Body image, peers and media affect eating behaviours.

NUTRITION

Adults: 21 to 65 Years

Physiologic changes, stress, pregnancy and menopause present nutritional challenges in adults. The risk of cancer, heart disease, stroke, diabetes and hypertension can be significantly lowered by modest changes in diet and exercise to reduce weight and change the body composition.

Adequate intake of fruits and vegetables, anti-oxidants, especially Vitamins A and C, whole grains and a reduction in saturated fat, cholesterol, and Trans fats reduces health risks.

Aging: Over 65 Years

Physical changes with aging result in less absorption of calcium, iron, folate, Vitamins B6 and B12 and less efficient production of Vitamin D.

Changes in taste and smell may lead to a decline of appetite and weight loss.

A less active body requires fewer calories but more nutrients. The need increases for fibre, fluids and protein.

Vitamins D, B12, A, and E, as well as folate, calcium and magnesium are important nutrients. Increase the intake of fruits and vegetables, whole grains and protein to address these needs.

Astonishing fact

Frozen vegetables can actually be healthier for you than fresh produce, since vegetables lose their nutrients as they wait to be eaten and freezing your vegetables stops that process.

Tips for a healthy diet

Food has undergone many changes as science and technology have progressed and many new aspects of food have been revealed. Nutrition took on a mantle of its own and today forms a very important part in dictating our daily food intake. No longer do most people just eat to live.

Nutrition has been classified into six major nutrition groups namely **carbohydrates**, **proteins**, **fats**, **vitamins**, **minerals** and water. Each one has a role to play in providing a balanced diet to the body.

Each food group has its own part to play in the overall diet of an individual. To avoid stomach disorders and other food related problems, such as indigestion and ulcers, one has to try and eat a balanced meal which contains as many food groups as possible. This is turn will lead to a balanced diet wherein all food ingested is nutritious and can be utilized by the body without any wastage.

Avoid starchy food, fatty foods, foods heavy in spices, and foods with additives wherever possible as these do not aid digestion. Similarly, an excess of salt and sugar would be harmful and the benefits that these foods normally provide would be lost. Every food item plays a small part in our overall nutrition and health. Anything that is too little or too much would upset the balance of the body and its system.

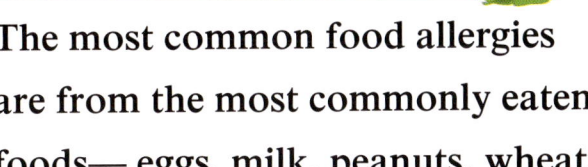

Astonishing fact

The most common food allergies are from the most commonly eaten foods— eggs, milk, peanuts, wheat, fish, and various nuts from trees.

NUTRITION

As with all other fields, food too has seen a lot of innovation and variety. Unfortunately, along with the good food there are also a whole range of foods which has a feel good factor to it but does nothing for the health of the person. These are called **empty calorie foods** in the form of soft drinks, various types of snacks, processed food, etc. Temptation is very difficult to resist so one must strike a balance wherein all desires for food are covered without compromising on the nutrition required by the body.

A good, balanced diet would ideally consist of a controlled intake of saturated and trans fats, cholesterol, sugar and salt, and meats, whilst eating enough fruits, vegetables, wholegrain products, low fat or normal fat dairy products, good fats such as fish, nuts and vegetable oils, fat-free meats, poultry and lentils. Last but not least, check the calorie count of the food on your plate. There is a lot of nutritional information available regarding the content of food and its calorific value. Investing in a guide and eating healthy food could pay rich dividends in future. Along with all this, a sustained and energetic exercise regime will go a long way to a healthy you.

Astonishing fact

Carrots were first cultivated for their medicinal uses and have in recent times been proven to not only improve the health of your eye tissues but your night vision as well.

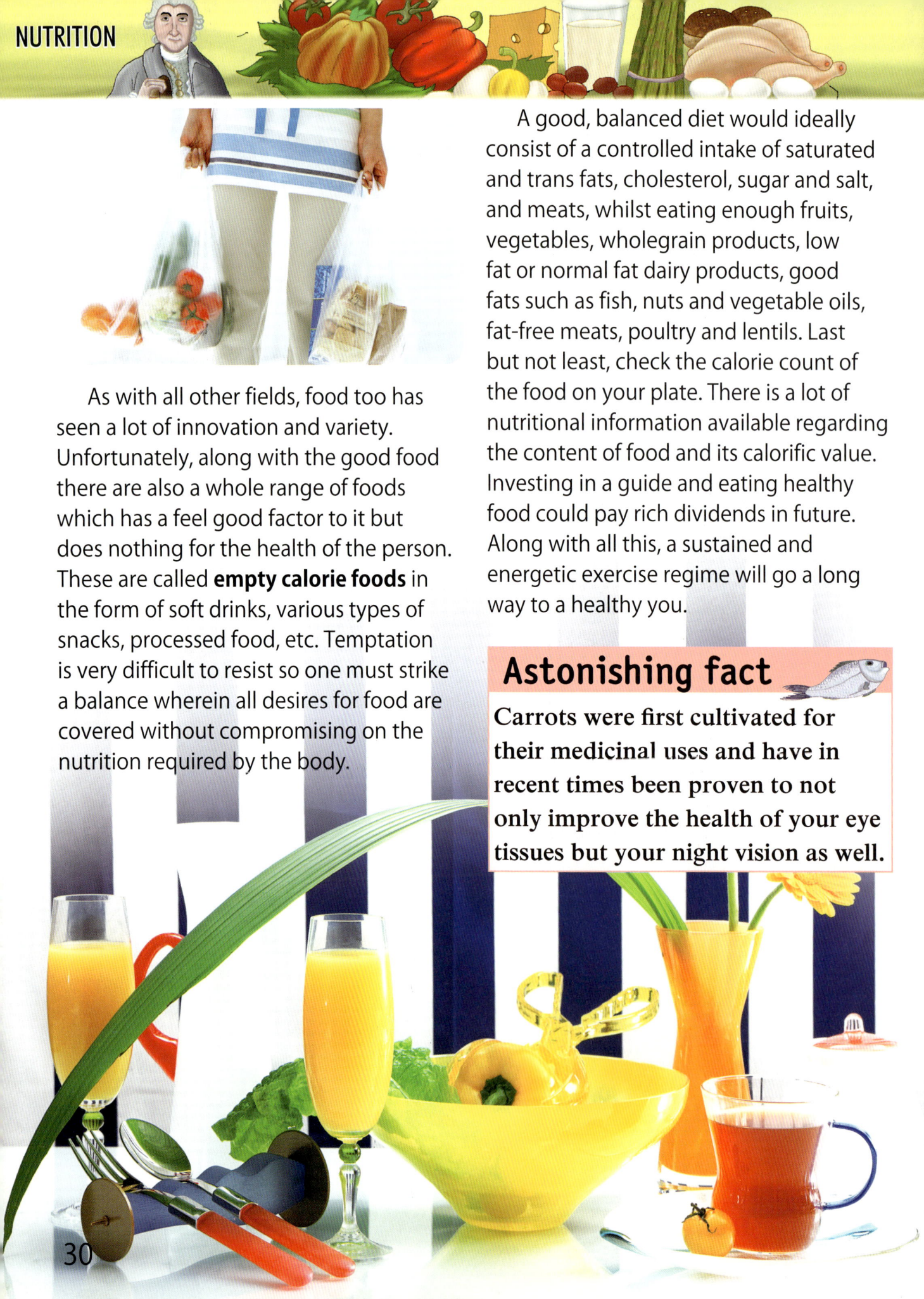

Test Your MEMORY

1. What is nutrition?

2. Write briefly about the history of nutrition.

3. Name the types of nutrients.

4. What is malnutrition?

5. What is plant nutrition?

6. What is animal nutrition?

7. What is human nutrition?

8. What is sports nutrition?

9. What are processed foods?

10. Why is proper nutrition important?

11. What are the dangers of poor nutrition?

12. Write some tips for a healthy diet.

Index

A

amino acids 12, 14, 16, 20, 21, 25
anaemia 15, 23
Antoine Lavoisier 6
aseptic processing 19

B

beriberi 15, 24

C

calcium 8, 12, 13, 16, 19, 20, 22, 27, 28
calories 15, 22, 28
canning 19
carbohydrates 7, 8, 14, 16, 17, 20, 22, 29

D

diabetes 15, 25, 28
diet 3, 4, 5, 8, 10, 11, 15, 16, 17, 18, 20, 21, 22, 23, 24, 25, 27, 28, 29, 30
dietician 17
dizziness 10
Dr James Lind 5

E

empty calorie foods 30

F

fats 7, 8, 14, 19, 21, 22, 25, 28, 29, 30
fatty acids 7, 16, 20
food allergies 4, 26, 29
food processing 19
freezing 19, 28
fruits 7, 13, 17, 21, 24, 25, 27, 28, 30

G

glucose 20, 21

H

human nutrition 14, 15

I

infants 26

L

limes 4, 5

M

macronutrients 12
magnesium 12, 16, 22, 27, 28
malnutrition 3, 4, 10, 11
metabolism 3, 5, 6
micronutrients 12
minerals 3, 8, 17, 19, 29

N

nitrogen 6, 12, 13, 16
nucleic acids 16
nutrients 3, 4, 7, 9, 10, 11, 14, 15, 21, 22, 23, 25, 26, 27, 28
nutrition 3, 5, 4, 10, 11, 12, 14, 15, 17, 18, 19, 20, 22, 26, 29, 30
nutritional science 17
nutritionist 17

O

obesity 15

P

Pellagra 24
phosphorous 12
plant nutrition 12
potassium 12, 13
proteins 8, 12, 14, 16, 27, 29

R

red blood cells 23
refrigeration 19
rickets 6, 9, 13, 23

S

scurvy 4, 5, 10, 15, 24
sports nutrition 17, 18
starvation 10, 11
sulphur 12, 13

T

toddlers 26

V

vegetables 16, 17, 19, 21, 24, 25, 27, 28, 30
Vitamin A 6, 9
Vitamin B 6
Vitamin D 5, 6, 9, 13, 23, 27, 28
vitamin pills 6
vitamins 3, 6, 9, 13, 14, 16, 19, 21, 22, 23, 27, 28, 29

W

water 6, 9, 12, 14, 15, 16, 17, 29